Buddha Stories on Stage

A Collection of Plays for Children

Julie Meighan

JemBooks

First published in 2019
by
JemBooks
Ireland
ISBN: 978-0-9935506-9-0

All rights reserved.

No part of this book may be reproduced or utilised in any form or by any electronic, digital or mechanical means, including information storage, photocopying, filming, recording, video recording and retrieval systems, without prior permission in writing from the publisher. The only exception is by a reviewer, who may quote short excerpts in a review. The moral rights of the author have been asserted.

Text Copyright © 2019, Julie Meighan

About the Author

Julie runs an educational blog at http://dramastartbooks.com where she writes about all aspects of drama in education. She has written several books for teachers on the subject. Her books have been translated into several languages including Hungarian and Chinese, and to date have sold over 40,000 copies. Julie is currently a lecturer in Drama at Cork Institute of Technology, Cork, Ireland where she lectures on the Early Years Education and Social Care degree courses. She has delivered drama workshops and training to a wide variety of academic and professional organisations worldwide. You can follow her on Twitter @drama_start.

Introduction:

This delightful collection of plays is based on famous Buddha stories. The plays are simple, so it is very easy for children to memorise their lines. The cast list is flexible – more characters can be added, and existing characters can be changed or omitted depending on the size and requirements of the group. The collection includes favourites such as *The Enlightenment of the Buddha*, The *Man and his Four Wives* and *The Buddha and the Beggar*. The scripts are simple and can be used as performance plays, reader's theatre or just read for enjoyment.

Props/costumes/stage directions:

There is a minimal number of props required to stage these plays. The costumes for all the plays are or can be very simple. For example, the children can just wear a colour that represents their animal, a mask or some face paint. A word of advice: if the children wear masks, make sure they don't cover their mouths as it would make it difficult to hear them speak. All suggestions for stage directions are included in brackets and italics.

I hope you enjoy performing or reading the following plays as much as my drama groups have over the years.

BREAK A LEG!

Contents

Information about Buddhism 1

Top 25 Buddha Inspiration Sayings 3

The Enlightenment of the Buddha 5

The Buddha and the Angry Man 9

The Buddha and the Poor Man 11

The Buddha and the Grieving Mother 12

The Final Days of the Buddha 14

The Buddha and the Beggar Man 16

The Man and his Four Wives 21

The Buffalo and the Monkey 24

The Greedy Crow 27

The Noble Monkey 29

The Foolish Vulture 32

The Buddha and Angulimala 35

A Cup of Tea 37

Buddhism was founded by Siddhartha Gautama (563 BC – 483 BC). A rich prince who was born in Lumbini, Nepal. He gave up his family, kingdom and all his material possessions to find a way to end suffering. After his death, his teachings and philosophy spread through Asian countries such as Tibet, Sri Lanka, China, Mongolia, Korea, and Japan and recently western countries have embraced Buddhism.

Buddhism teaches people how to end their suffering by eliminating greed, hatred and ignorance in their lives. It believes that negative actions have negative consequences and positive actions have positive consequences. This is known as karma. Karma is reflected in the endless cycles of life, death and rebirth. Buddhism believes in reincarnation (rebirth). The ultimate goal of a Buddhist is to reach the state of enlightenment (Nirvana) and free oneself from endless reincarnation and suffering.

Life involves suffering. The reason for this suffering is that we want things we cannot or do not have. More importantly, we become attached to wanting things we cannot or do not have. The way to cure suffering is to stop the wanting. Many could argue that a better way would simply be to go get the thing you want. The Buddhist response is that we can never get everything we want, partly because the more we have, the more we want.

The way to stop wanting is to follow the *Noble Eightfold Path*, which focuses not on changing things around us, but instead it focuses on changing our own mind on how we view things.

Four Noble Truth

The four noble truths are considered the first teaching of the Buddha.

Noble Truth 1: Life is full of suffering.

Noble Truth 2: Suffering comes from wanting.

Noble Truth 3: Suffering stops when wanting stops.

Noble Truth 4: In order to stop wanting follow the Noble Eightfold path.

Noble Eightfold Path

The Buddha told people to follow a special way of life called the Noble Eightfold Path.

These are:

- Know and understand the Four Noble Truths
- Give up all worldly things and don't harm others
- Tell the truth, don't gossip, and don't talk badly about others
- Don't commit evil acts, like killing, stealing, or living an unclean life
- Work for good and oppose evil
- Do rewarding work
- Make sure your mind keeps your senses under control
- Practice meditation as a way of understanding reality

Top 25 Buddha Inspiration Sayings

In the end, only three things matter: How much you loved, how gently you lived, and how gracefully you let go of things not meant for you.

When the student is ready, the teacher will appear.

The less you respond to negative people, the more peaceful your life will become.

Do not learn how to react learn how to respond.

Holding onto anger is like drinking poison and expecting the other person to die.

What you think you, become, what you feel, you attract, what you imagine, you create.

If you want to fly, give up everything that weighs you down.

Nothing can harm you as much as your own thoughts unguarded.

The whole secret of existence is to have no fear.

It is during our darkest moments that we must focus to see the light.

Be patient everything comes to you in the right moment.

Each morning we are born again. What we do today is what matters most.

It is better to be hated for what you are than to be loved for what you are not.

He who does not understand your silence will probably not understand your words.

Happiness does not depend on what you have or who you are it solely relies on what you think.

The secret of health for both mind and body is not to mourn for the past, nor to worry about the future, but to live the present moment wisely and earnestly.

Holding on to anger is like grasping a hot coal with the intent of throwing it at someone else; you are the one who gets burned.

People with opinions just go around bothering one another.

An insincere and evil friend is more to be feared than a wild beast; a wild beast may wound your
body, but an evil friend will wound your mind.

A dog is not considered a good dog because he is a good barker. A man is not considered a good man because he is a good talker.

Everything changes, nothing remains without change.

Thousands of candles can be lighted from a single candle, and the life of the candle will not be shortened.

Happiness never decreases by being shared.

It is better to travel well than to arrive.

Even death is not to be feared by one who has lived wisely.

The Enlightenment of the Buddha

Characters: Storyteller, Wise man, King, Queen, Prince Siddhartha/Buddha, servant, old man, old woman, mother, father, beggar man, five holy men, young woman, Mara, Mara's daughter.

Storyteller: Prince Siddhartha was born on the full moon to loving parents.

(King and queen are cradling the baby and a wise man enters.)

Wise Man: He will grow up to be a king or a great leader.

King: I do not want him to become a wandering fortune-teller.

Queen: Our son shall never see the horrors of the world.

King: That is a good idea. If he never sees pain and suffering, he will never see the need of religion.

Prince Siddhartha grew up but he was never satisfied. He had many questions to ask.

Prince Siddhartha: What is life? I wonder what is behind the palace walls. *(He rings a bell and a servant walk in and bows.)*

Servant: Yes, master you called?

Prince Siddhartha: I want to go outside the palace walls.

Servant: I will call the carriage.

(The carriage comes in and the Prince Siddhartha and servant climb on board. They ride through the town.)

Prince Siddhartha: I want to see what this place is really like. STOP the carriage.

(Prince Siddhartha jumps off the carriage and ran through the streets.)

Servant: Come back. *(Prince Siddhartha disappears into the streets and the carriages continues on without him.)*

Storyteller: He was horrified by what he saw an old woman who was toothless and crooked.

Prince Siddhartha: What is the matter with you?

Old Woman: I am old. *(She gives him a confusing look.)* Have you never seen an old person before?

(Prince Siddhartha shakes his head.)

Storyteller: Then he came across a man

Prince Siddhartha: What is the matter with you?

Old man: I have been eaten up by disease. I am waiting to die.

Storyteller: Then he saw a funeral procession

Prince Siddhartha: What is this?

Mother: Our son has died of disease.

Father: His body will be burned on the pyre.

Prince Siddhartha: What's suffering there is outside the palaces' walls, I had no idea.

(He then saw an old man begging for alms.)

Prince Siddhartha: What are you doing? You look so poor you must be miserable.

Beggar man: No, I am happy and I am at peace.

Prince Siddhartha: This must be the answer.

Storyteller: Prince Siddhartha returned the palace and packed his bags.

Servant: Where are you going?

Buddha: I am leaving these palace walls for good.

Servant: But why are you wearing orange rags?

Buddha: I no longer need nice clothes and material things.

Storyteller: Prince Siddhartha went to the far ends of the kingdom he met five holy men.

Prince Siddhartha: Why are you naked and dirty?

Holy men: If you make your body suffer, your mind can grow and your spirit can be free.

Buddha: I will join you and starve myself, maybe I will get some answers.

Storyteller: He sat in the forest suffering for days.

Prince Siddhartha: It has been 49 days. A new idea is forming. Life can never satisfy us because we want more. I must stay like this forever.

Storyteller: Prince Siddhartha ate very little he was burnt by the sun and frozen by the winter. Six long years past without food or drink.

Prince Siddhartha: I do not think I am any nearer to my goal. I still do not know the way to put an end to suffering. I wasted so much time.

Storyteller: One day a young woman passed by Prince Siddhartha

Young Woman: I can see someone sitting in stillness, his face is shining radiance. *(She stops.)* Here eat some of my food. *(He accepts the food and eats it.)*

Prince Siddhartha: Thank you for the food, your offering has given me the strength to find the truth. My strength has returned. *(The young woman leaves and waves goodbye.)*

Storyteller: Prince Siddhartha sat on the ground under the Bodhi tree.

Prince Siddhartha: I will not get up from this tree until I reach my goal.

Storyteller: Mara, the demon of death and evil was not happy. *(Mara suddenly appears.)*

Mara: Look at him. If he reaches enlightenment before me, I will lose my evil power. I must disturb him or I am doomed for eternity. What shall I do? I know I will make storms and lightning. Let us shoot poisonous arrows at him.

Storyteller: The bad weather did not bother Prince Siddhartha. The poisonous arrows did not make the prince move.

Mara: I am getting desperate. I know I will call my daughter. Daughter, come here at once.

Mara's Daughter: Yes, Father, what do you want?

Mara: I have turned you into a beautiful woman. I want to dance in front of the prince and make him move. *(Music plays and Mara's daughter starts to dance.)*

Storyteller: Mara's daughter danced in front of Prince Siddhartha but even a beautiful woman could not disturb him.

Mara's daughter: I have tried everything nothing works.

Storyteller: Mara was defeated miserably

Mara: You are wasting your life and my time. I cannot be bothered anymore. I am off. *(Mara disappears.)*

Prince Siddhartha: The Earth is my witness.

Storyteller: Gradually his concentration deepened. Desire is the true cause. Once the heart is free of desire will be fully of happiness. He was now the Buddha. The enlightened one. The world is full of peace and happiness

Buddha: I shall teach and begin my word.

There are four noble truths.

The truth of suffering.

The truth of the cause of suffering.

The truth of the end of suffering.

The truth of the path that leads to the end of suffering.

The Buddha and the Angry Man

(How to handle an insult)

Characters: Storyteller, Buddha, Angry Man.

Storyteller: One day, the Buddha was walking from village to village to spread love and compassionate. *(He walks slowly, looking around taking in the wonders of his surroundings.)*

Buddha: What a lovely, sunny day it is for a walk.

(Suddenly, an angry man runs towards him, waving his fists.)

Angry Man: Who do you think you are?

Buddha: Whatever is the matter?

Angry Man: You, that is what the matter is, you walk around, thinking you know everything to teach goodness and love. You are just a fake, silly man in an orange robe.

Buddha: Come sit with me. *(He guides towards a tree and they sit in the shade.)*

Angry Man: *(confused)* Why are you not angry at my insult?

Buddha: I have a question for you.

Angry Man: What?

Buddha: If you buy a present for someone and that person, doesn't want it then whom does the present belong to?

Angry Man: What a strange question. Me, of course, I bought the present.

Buddha: That's right and it's exactly the same with your anger.

Angry Man: That makes no sense.

Buddha: It is very clear, if you become angry with me and I do not accept your anger then it falls back on you and all you succeed in doing is hurt yourself more.

Angry Man: What should I do?

Buddha: Rid yourself of your anger and become a more a loving person.

Angry Man: I will try. Thank you for teaching me this lesson. *(They hug and wave goodbye to one another.)*

Storyteller: The moral of story is when you have hate and anger towards other people only you are unhappy

The Buddha and the Poor Man

Characters: Storyteller, Buddha and Poor Man.

Storyteller: One day the Buddha was walking through a village. He met a poor man.

(Enters Poor Man begging.)

Poor Man: Buddha, I have a question for you.

Buddha: Yes, Poor Man. What is it you want to ask me?

Poor Man: Well I was wondering why am I so poor?

Buddha: The answer is simple.

Poor Man: It is, please tell me.

Buddha: If you learned to give, you would not be so poor.

Poor Man: Look at me. I have nothing to give. I am a very poor man.

Buddha: Well, first of all you can smile, be cheerful and happy. Then, you can speak kind words and give comfort to people.

Poor Man: What else could I give?

Buddha: You can look at people with empathy and kindness and you can physically help others.

Poor Man: So, I am not a poor man after all.

Buddha: You are only ever poor when you are poor in your heart.

Storyteller: The poor man thanked the Buddha and went on his way a rich man.

The Buddha and the Grieving Mother

Characters: Storyteller, Buddha, Mother, Three neighbours.

Storyteller: Once when Buddha was sitting quietly under a Bodhi tree, a woman approached him. She was very sad.
(Woman walks towards Buddha, she is crying.)
Buddha: Why are you looking sad?
Mother: I hear you are a great holy man who performs great miracles. I lost my son this morning. Please bring him back and help me out of my grief.
Buddha: I will help you but first you must do something for me.
Woman: I will do anything to get my son back.
Buddha: Bring me some mustard seeds from a house where no one has died.
Woman: Is that all I have to do? That will be easy.
(Woman walks off and goes to her neighbour. She knocks on the door.)
Neighbour 1: Hello, how may I help you?
Mother: Has anyone died in this house?
Neighbour 1: Yes, my sister died two years ago.
Mother: I am very sorry to hear that. *(She hugs the neighbour.)* I will be on my way.
(She walks to the second neighbour and knocks on the door.)
Neighbour 2: Hello, how may I help you?
Mother: Has anyone died in this house?
Neighbour 2: Yes, my father died six months ago.
Mother: I am very sorry to hear that. *(She hugs the neighbour.)* I will

be on my way.

(She walks to the third neighbour and knocks on the door.)

Neighbour 3: Hello, how may I help you?

Mother: Has anyone died in this house?

Neighbour 3: Yes, my daughter died three day ago.

Mother: I am very sorry to hear that. *(She hugs the neighbour).* I will be on my way.

Mother: What shall I do? How disappointing I cannot find mustard seeds from a house where no one has died.

(She goes back to the Buddha who is still sitting quietly under the Bodhi tree.)

Buddha: Where are you mustard seeds?

Mother: I could not find them but I have realised I am not the only one who has experienced death.

Buddha: You have learned a very valuable lesson today. Death comes to everyone in the end.

The Final Days of the Buddha

Characters: Storyteller, Buddha, four followers (you can have as many followers as you need).

Storyteller: The Buddha gave his teachings to everyone who is interested and listened.

(Buddha walks on the stage. He is old and frail and walks very slowly.)

Buddha: I am eighty years old. I have spread knowledge, peace, love and happiness. Now I must show everyone how to leave this world peacefully and without fear.

Buddha: Followers, come here. *(All his followers walk on to the stage.)*

Follower 1: Yes, Buddha, you called.

Follower 2: How may we help you?

Buddha: We must return to Kushinga for the last time: I wish to die in a city where I grew up.

Follower 3: Buddha, you cannot die.

Follower 4: What would we do without you?

Buddha: I have always taught you that death was the final part of life. It is nothing to fear. Now let us go.

Storyteller: They travelled for many days. *(They all look tired and hungry.)*

Follower 1: We have reached a village we should stop and rest.

Buddha: I am tired. I will lie down between these two trees.

Storyteller: The Buddha laid down between the two trees and his followers gathered around him.

Follower 1: He cannot die.

Follower 2: You must not worry; his teachings will live on.

Follower 3: They will be our guide.

Follower 4: We cannot do it by ourselves.

Buddha: *(wakes up)* Remember what I taught you. Craving and desires are the root causes of all unhappiness. Everything changes so it is important you do not become attached to anything. Focus your mind and find lasting happiness. Now I must sleep.

Storyteller: The Buddha turned in his side and passed away peacefully. It was a full moon.

On every full moon night the followers of Buddha would gather together to chant his teachings.

The Buddha and the Beggar Man

Characters: Two storytellers, Beggar Man, Mouse, Man, Woman, Daughter, Wizard, Giant Turtle and Buddha.

Storyteller 1: Once upon a time there was a homeless man who begged every day for food.

(People pass by and give him food.)

Beggar Man: I am so lucky that kind people give me food.

(Beggar Man falls asleep and mouse creeps up and steals his food. The Beggar Man wakes up suddenly and sees the mouse.)

Beggar Man: Mouse, why are you stealing my food? I am just a poor beggar man.

Mouse: I am doing you a favour because no matter how much you beg or how generous people are; you will never be allowed to keep more than eight items.

Beggar Man: Who has decided that I cannot own more than eight items?

Mouse: The Buddha has decided.

Beggar Man: But why me?

Mouse: Why don't you go find him and ask him.

(Mouse scampers off with the food.)

Beggar Man: Well, I had better go find the Buddha and ask him why I am not allowed to possess more than eight items.

Storyteller 2: So the beggar man gathered his few belongings and went on a journey to find the Buddha.

Storyteller 1: He travelled all day. As night fell, he grew cold and hungry.

Beggar Man: There is no sign of the Buddha. I am tired and hungry. There is a light over there. Perhaps if I knock on the door, they may let me stay for the night.

(He knocks on the door. A man opens the door with a warm smile.)

Beggar Man: I am cold and hungry; please can I stay the night?

Man: Of course, please come in.

Woman: Sit down and have some food with us.

(He enters the house and sits down on a table with the Man, woman and their daughter.)

Man: Where are you going at this time at night?

Beggar Man: I am going to find the Buddha. I have a very important question to ask him. I just need a good night's sleep and I will be on my way early in the morning.

(Man and woman look at each other.)

Woman: We have a question for you to ask the Buddha.

Man: Our daughter cannot speak. Please ask the Buddha what we need to do hear her beautiful voice.

Beggar Man: Of course, I will ask the Buddha your question. Thanks you for the food and bed.

Storyteller 2: The beggar man continues on his way and his quest to find the Buddha.

Storyteller 1: He comes across a range of mountains.

Beggar Man: Oh dear, the mountains look to difficult to climb but I really need to find the Buddha to ask my questions.

(He starts to climb the mountains.)

Beggar Man: This is very difficult. I will never make it. *(He sits downs and starts to weep.)*

(Enters wizard.)

Wizard: What is the matter, young man? Why are you crying?

Beggar Man: I have very important questions to ask the Buddha but I cannot climb these mountains. I will never find him now.

Wizard: I will help you. We can use my magic to fly over the mountain come with me.

Storyteller 2: Wizard used his staff's magic to fly the beggar man and himself across the mountains.

Beggar Man: Thank you so much, wizard. I would have never made if it were not for you.

Wizard: You are welcome, but can I ask you a favour.

Beggar Man: Of course, I'll do anything to show my gratitude.

Wizard: Can you ask the Buddha what I have to do to get to heaven. I have been trying to get there for a thousand years.

(The beggar man nods his head, they hug, and the wizard hops on his staff and flies off.)

Storyteller 1: The beggar man continues on his journey and comes across a river.

Beggar Man: I do not believe this. How am I going to get across the river? *(He sighs.)*

(Enters Giant Turtle.)

Giant Turtle: You look sad. What is the matter?

Beggar Man: I have a very important question to ask the Buddha and I cannot get across the river to find him.

Giant Turtle: Jump on my back and I will swim across. *(The beggar man jumps on the Giant Turtle's back and they swim across the river.)*

Beggar Man: Thank you, Giant Turtle. How can I repay you?

Giant Turtle: Can you ask the Buddha a question for me?

Beggar Man: Of course, what is your question?

Giant Turtle: Ask the Buddha why I have not become a dragon. I have been trying to become a dragon for 500 years.

(Beggar Man nods and hugs the giant turtle.)

Storyteller 2: Eventually the beggar man finds the Buddha under the Bodhi Tree.

Beggar Man: I am so glad. I have found you. I have so many question to ask you.

Buddha: I will only answer three questions.

Beggar Man: But I have four questions to ask and them all very important.

Buddha: Ask yourself, are they equally important?

Storyteller 1: The beggar man thought very carefully.

Beggar Man: Well, the giant turtle is trying to be a dragon for fifty years. The wizard has trying to go to heaven for 1000 years. The young girl will be unable to speak for the rest of her life if I do not ask her question. I am just a homeless beggar. I can go back and continue begging. My question is the least important by far.

(Beggar Man goes back to the Buddha.)

Beggar Man: My first question is how can the turtle become a dragon?

Buddha: Simple, he needs to leave the comfort of his own shell, unless he does that he will never be a dragon.

Beggar Man: My second question is how can the wizard go to heaven?

Buddha: He must put down his magic staff as it keeps him on earth. The moment he puts it down he will be free to go to heaven.

Beggar Man: My third question how can the young girl speak.

Buddha: She will speak when she meets her soulmate.

Beggar Man: Thank you for answering my questions.

Storyteller 2: The beggar man turned around and started his journey home. He meets the Giant Turtle.

Giant Turtle: Hey Beggar man, did you ask the Buddha my question?

Beggar Man: Of course I did. The answer is simple. Take off your shell and you will become a dragon.

(Giant Turtle takes off his shell.)

Giant Turtle: I have these priceless pearls in my shell. Here take them. I will not need them anymore because I am a dragon. Goodbye and good luck.

(The dragon flies off.)

(Enters the wizard.)

Wizard: Did you ask the Buddha my question?

Beggar Man: Of course I did. The answer is simple. Put your staff down and you can go to heaven.

Wizard: Here take my staff, Use its power wisely. Thank you.

(The wizard ascends into heaven.)

Beggar Man: Now, I have wealth from the turtle and power from the wizard. He hops on the staff and makes his way back tom the family that gave him food and shelter.

Man: Hello, did you ask the Buddha our question?

Beggar Man: Of course I did. The answer is simple. Your daughter will speak when she meets her soulmate.

Daughter: Hello, you are the man that was here last week.

Woman: Looks like you found your soulmate.

(Daughter and beggar man hug.)

Storytellers: The moral of the story if you do good, you will be repaid.

The Man and his Four Wives

Characters: Two Storytellers, Old Man, Wife 1, Wife 2, Wife 3, Wife 4.

Storyteller 1: Once there was a man with four wives

Storyteller 2: The man was ill and about to die. . *(An old man is lying on his bed and his four wives walk on the stage.)*

Wife 1: Our husband is very old and ill. *(The four wives walk over to the old man.)*

Wife 2: You must eat something.

Wife 3: It will make you stronger. *(She tries to give the man some food but he refuses.)*

Wife 4: We do not want you to die.

Old Man: I am coming to the end of my life I do not want to die. Wife 1, I have loved you all my life and I have always taken care of you. Please, come with me wherever I go after death.

Wife 1: My dear husband, I know you have always loved me, but now it is time for us to go our separate ways. Goodbye my dear. *(She kisses him on the forehead and leaves).*

Old Man: That is disappointing; luckily, I have three more wives.

Storyteller 1: He calls his second wife.

Old Man: Wife 2, please come here.

Wife 2: Yes, my dear how can I help?

Old Man: I am coming to the end of my life I do not want to die. Wife 2, I have loved you all my life and I have always taken care of you. Please, come with me wherever I go after death.

Wife 2: My dear husband, I know you have always loved me, but now it is time for me to find a new husband. Goodbye my dear. *(She kisses him on the forehead and leaves).*

Old Man: That is disappointing; luckily, I have two more wives.

Storyteller 2: He calls his third wife.

Old Man: Wife 3, please come here.

Wife 3: Yes, my dear how can I help?

Old Man: I am coming to the end of my life I do not want to die. Wife 3, I have loved you all my life and I have always taken care of you. Please, come with me wherever I go after death.

Wife 3: I am sorry you are dying. I will go with you to the cemetery but I will have to leave you there and continue with the rest of my life.

Old Man: That is disappointing, I have a fourth wife.

Storyteller: He calls to his fourth wife.

Old Man: Wife 4, please come here.

Wife 4: Yes, my dear how can I help you?

Old Man: I have never really treated you very well. I have always treated you liked a slave. If I asked you to come with me after death, you will probably say no. But I am so lonely and terrified of life after death, please come with me wherever I go after death.

Fourth Wife: Of course, I will come with you. My dear husband, I will always be with you whatever happens.

Old Man: Thank you, I feel so sad I've neglected you all my life. I wish I treated you better when I was young and healthy.

Storyteller: The old man closed his eyes and died.

(The four wives walk to the front of the stage.)

Four wives: Every man/woman has four wives/four husbands.

First wife: The first wife is the body. During our lifetime we love our body and everything it craves. However, our body can't follow us in death.

Second wife: The second wife represents material things such as wealth and fame which other get when we die.

Third wife: The third wife is the relationship we have with our family friends and society. While saddened by our deaths there is nothing they can do. We are born alone and we die alone.

Fourth wife: The four wife represents the conscious mind. She will follow us wherever we go.

The Buffalo and the Monkey

Characters: Two Storyteller, Buffalo, Monkey, Mouse and as many jungle animals as you want in the background.

Storyteller 1: Once upon a time the Buddha who lived as a great being, came back to earth as a buffao. *(Buffalo walks on the stage proudly, showing his muscles.)* He was a sight to behold. He had big, bulging muscles and a powerful presence. All the other animals in the jungle feared him because they knew they could not match his strength.

Buffalo: *(addresses the audience)* I may look fierce on the outside but on the inside I'm compassionate and wise. *(Monkey walks on the stage and sees the buffalo.)*

Monkey: There is the Buffalo, all the animals fear him. I know that he would never hurt anyone. He is full of kindness. I think, I will play a trick on him.

Storyteller 2: The monkey jumped up on the buffalo's back, grab his horns and started to ride him like a horse. *(Monkey jumps on the buffalo's back.)*

Monkey: Giddy up, Horsey.

Buffalo: *(sighs)* You do know, Monkey, I'm buffalo and not a horse.

Monkey: Of course, I know you are a buffalo. But this is fun.

Storyteller 1: When the Buffalo went to the lake to take a drink, the monkey played another trick on him.

Monkey: I'm going to cover the Buffalo's eyes so he can see.

Storyteller 2: The monkey covered the Buffalo eyes and soon the Buffalo fell into the river.

(Monkey laughs and the buffalo struggles to get out of the river.)

Buffalo: Monkey, no matter what you do to me I will never get angry.

Monkey: I'm only playing tricks on you. It's fun.

Storyteller 1: Every night while the Buffalo was sleeping. The monkey would wake him up.

(The monkey tiptoes up to the buffalo while he is sleeping and wakes him up.)

Monkey: No matter, what I do to the Buffalo he never gets angry at me he just goes about his business.

Storyteller 2: One day, a little mouse who lives in jungle decided to ask the Buffalo why he never gets angry with the monkey. *(Little mouse scampers up to the buffalo.)*

Mouse Buffalo, everyone in this jungle fears you. You are so big and strong but yet you let the monkey play tricks on you every day. I don't understand why you don't get angry.

Buffalo: My dear mouse, this something I have to tell you. Anger never leads to happiness so you see the monkey is doing me a favour.

Mouse: A favour? I don't understand. How does a monkey who plays tricks on you every day do you a favour?

Buffalo: Every time, the monkey plays a trick on me I work on developing patience and compassion. When I am patient and compassionate I feel peaceful inside.

Mouse: I'm still confused the monkey's tricks will get worse if you don't teach a lesson.

Buffalo: My patience is the lesson. He may be a silly monkey but like everyone, he has a heart.

Mouse: But no animal in the jungle likes the monkey, they don't like his tricks and no one wants to be friends with him.

Buffalo: Yes, I know none of the animals want him around and everyone pushes them away. They're sick of his tricks. He has no friends except for me because he is helping me to grow.

Mouse: Buffalo, you may be strong and fierce but you are wise and compassionate. Thank you for teaching me this lesson. Maybe someday I will learn to have patience like you. *(The little mouse scampers off and the monkey is hiding behind a tree).*

Storyteller 1: What the buffalo did not know, was that the monkey was hiding behind a tree. He heard with the Buffalo had set the mouse. *(The monkey comes out slowly from behind the tree.)*

Monkey: Buffalo: thank you for being my friend. I will no longer play tricks on you or the other animals in the jungle. *(They hug each other.)*

The Greedy Crow

Characters: Storyteller, Crow, Kingfisher, Hawk.

Storyteller: One day a crow found a piece of meat. (*He picks up the meat. He is beaming because he can't believe his luck.*)

Crow: What luck? I found a juicy piece of meat. I will fly up on to the tree and eat it all by myself. (*He points up to a tree and flies up there.*).

Storyteller: While he was sitting on the tree about to eat his juicy piece of meat, a small silvery kingfisher passed by. (*Kingfisher has something in his mouth.*)

Crow: Hello Kingfisher, What do you have there?

(*The kingfisher removes the object from his mouth.*)

Kingfisher: A dead rat. I'm going to eat it for my supper.

Crow: Stop and give me a piece of the dead rat.

Kingfisher: Why would I do that? The rat is mine besides you have a juicy piece of meat in front of you. Be happy with what you have. I'm off home.

Crow: Come back here at once, kingfisher. If you don't give me some dead rat, I shall chase you and take it all for myself.

Kingfisher: Ha, ha, I'd like to see you try.

Storyteller: The crow dropped his juicy piece of meat and chased after the kingfisher. Although the kingfisher was a small bird but he could fly much faster than the crow. Soon a hawk landed on the tree and saw the crow's piece of meat.

Hawk: What's this? A nice juicy piece of meat. What luck I have? I'll eat it for my dinner.

Crow: Kingfisher, come back here.

(*Kingfisher turns around waves to crow and flies off laughing. The crow stops chasing him. He is very tired.)*

Crow: The kingfisher was too fast for me. I'll fly back to my tree and have my juicy piece of meabt.

(He flies back to the tree. He sees the hawk perched on the branch but there is no sign of the meat. The hawk is licking his lips.)

Crow: Excuse me, Mr. Hawk but did you see a juicy piece anywhere?

Hawk: I've eaten it. You must always remember Crow, it doesn't pay to be greedy.

(The Crow bows his head in despair. The hawk licks is lips and flies up into the sky looking very pleased with himself.)

The Noble Monkey

Characters: Storyteller, Monkey King, four Monkeys, Royal washerwoman, King, 2 soldiers.

Storyteller: Once upon a time, the monkey king called a meeting of all the monkeys in the jungle.
Monkey King: I have called this meeting to tell you it is very important not to let a mango fall into the river.
Monkey 1: Why not?
King: If you drop a mango into the river, the river will carry the mangos to humans and we do not want that.
Monkey 2: Why is that bad?
King: If the humans taste the mangoes, they will want more; they will search for the fruit and destroy our jungle.
Monkey 3: We will be very careful
Storyteller: The monkeys were very careful until one day…
(Monkey four trips over a rock and the mango falls into the river)
Monkey 4: Oh dear, I tripped and the mango has fallen into the river. Help me.
Storyteller: The monkeys tried to stop the mango but they failed miserably.
(The monkeys come out of the river. They look very upset.)
Storyteller: A few days later, a royal washerwoman was washing the king's clothes by the riverbank.
Royal Washerwoman: What is this? It looks like a juicy, sweet fruit. I will take it to the king.
King: Have you washed all my clothes?
Royal Washerwoman: Yes, your majesty and I found this sweet, juicy fruit on the riverbank. I would like you to have it. *(She gives*

him the mango and curtesys.)

King: Thank you, what an interesting looking fruit. I have never seen anything like this before. *(He bites into it.)* This is the sweetest fruit I have ever tasted. I need to find more. Soldiers, come here at once.

(Two soldiers enter.)

Soldier 1: Yes your majesty.

Soldier 2: How may we help you?

King: The royal washerwoman found the most delicious fruit on the riverbank. It must have floated down the river. We should look for more.

Soldiers: We will prepare the boat.

Storyteller: The king and soldiers set sail down the river. Soon they came across lots and lots of mango tree.

King: I knew we would find It., now we will have enough delicious fruit forever.

Monkey 1: Look it is humans on a boat.

Monkey 2: They must have found the mango.

Monkey 3: We must tell the monkey king quick.

Monkey 4: Monkey King, the humans are coming. They found the mango that I dropped into the water.

Monkey King: We must get out of here quickly. Jump on the vines and get to the other side of the riverbank we will be able to hide in the jungle.

Monkey 1: Come with us.

Monkey King: I will follow you once everyone is safe.

Monkey 2: We are all safe now. Jump on the vine and come quickly.

Storyteller: The monkey king jumped on the vine. The vine broke and the monkey king fell into the water. The king watched him from the boat.

King: The monkey king is very brave. He put all the other monkeys' safety before his own. He is a true king. We must rescue him at once.

Storyteller: The soldiers pulled the monkey king to safety.

King: Monkey King, I am very impressed by your bravery. All the other monkeys are safe. Come to my palace and stay for a few days so you can recover.

Monkey King: King, thank you for your kind invitation but my place is here with my subjects.

King: I had come here to get the mangoes but now I shall not touch them. Please continue to live here in peace.

Monkey King: Thank you so much for sparing my Kingdom and saving my life. Please take some of these golden juicy mangoes every year, I will send mangoes to your palace every month so you will never be without them.

Storyteller: They said goodbye and all the monkeys lived peacefully in the jungle. The moral of the story is be kind to others and they will be kind to you.

The Foolish Vulture

Characters: Storyteller, Old Vulture, Yellow Bird, Orange Bird, Green Bird, Blue Bird, Pink Bird, Black Bird, Cat, and young birds (as many as wanted).

Storyteller: Once upon a time, there was a hill that sloped down to the banks of a river. At the bottom of the hill, there was a neem tree which made the shelter for many birds. In a tree not far off there lived an old vulture who was half blind and didn't have a nest.

Old Vulture: Look at all those young birds living in the neem tree. They look like they are having such fun, I'd wish they let me join them.

Storyteller: One day a yellow bird flew by the old vulture's tree.

Yellow Bird: Old Vulture, you look sad. Whatever is the matter?

Old Vulture: I'm sitting her alone with no friends. I'm very lonely. *(The yellow bird gives the old vulture a hug and flies away.)*

Storyteller: The yellow bird flew back to the neem tree to speak to his friends about the vulture.

Yellow Bird: Friends, do you know the vulture in the next tree?

Orange Bird: Yes, he is very strange.

Green Bird: He looks so sad. What is the matter with him?

Yellow Bird: He is old, half blind and very lonely.

Blue Bird: What shall we do to help him?

Yellow Bird: We should invite him to live in our neem tree?

Pink Bird: Of course.

Orange Bird: But he is a vulture.

Yellow Bird: He is blind, he can't harm us.

Black Bird: Let's ask him to join us in the neem tree.

Storyteller: All the birds flew to the old vulture's tree.

Old Vulure: Hello, birds. What a pleasant surprise. Why are you here?

Yellow Bird: We would like you to come and live with us in our neem tree.

Pink Bird: You can share our food.

Black Bird: We will give you a nest of your own.

Orange Bird: And you can enjoy our company.

Old Vulture: I'll be delighted to come live with you. Thank you for your kindness.

Storyteller: The next day, the old vulture went to the neem tree and made it his home. The other birds fed him and he played with the young birds. One day a cat saw the old vulture on the tree.

Cat: Great sir, I'm delighted to see you here. You are the largest and most fierce of all birds. You are the king of all birds.

Old Vulture: Thank you but who are you. I can't see. I'm half blind.

Cat: I'm a cat.

Old Vulture: Go away. You are not welcome here.

Cat: Sir, listen to me first. You are a powerful bird that needs meat. The birds can only get you fruits and nuts.

Old Vulture: I don't want anything from you.

Storyteller: The cat left but he came back every day for a month. Each time he came he brought the old vulture meat. One day while the cat was chatting to the vulture. The Black bird returned to the tree. He waited for the cat to leave and then asked the vulture.

Black Bird: Why is the cat coming here, he is a danger to the young birds.

Old Vulture: He is a poor cat that just wants to be friends.

Black bird: Cats are very clever, keep him away from our tree. All the birds trust you with the young birds.

Old Vulture: I'm older than you and I know who to trust and whom not to trust.

Storyteller: The black bird flew off. The cat kept coming. One day while the vulture was sleeping the cat ate one of the baby birds and threw the bones in the old vulture's nest. When the birds came back they began looking for the baby bird.

Birds: Baby bird, where are you?

Orange Bird: Look, I found bones in the old vultures nest.

(Birds all rushed to the nest.)

Yellow Bird: Vulture, we trusted you but you have betrayed us.

Pink Bird: You have shown your true colours.

Blue Bird: Get out of our tree and don't come back.

Old Vulture: Friends, I didn't do anything. I was asleep.

Black Bird: I saw a cat talking to the vulture, perhaps it was him.

Birds: He invited cat here. Old Vulture leave our comfortable, safe home at once.

Storyteller: The birds drove the vulture from the nest. The vulture was in tears. He went back to his old tree.

Black Bird: Wrong friendships will always lead to bad things in life.

The Buddha and Angulimala

Characters: Storyteller, Buddha, Angulimala and the woman.

Storyteller: One day the Buddha came to a village. He noticed something was very strange.

Buddha: The streets are empty. Where is everyone? Hello? Hello anyone home?

(Then, he sees a woman hurrying by.)

Buddha: Excuse me, why are you in such a rush, where are all the villagers?

Woman: Have you not heard? Angulimala is on the prowl. Everyone has left the village for safety.

Buddha: Who is Angulimala?

Woman: He is a terrible killer. Everyone is afraid of him including the king and his soldiers.

Buddha: I wonder why Angulimala makes everyone and unhappy. I must find him and talk to him.

Storyteller: Angulimala was sitting outside his cave. He was admiring his finger necklace.

Angulimala: I've 99 fingers on my necklace. Fingers I've chopped off people I've killed. I need to find one finger to make my necklace complete. I wonder who will be my next victim.

(Buddha walks past.)

Angulimala: I'll get one of his fingers to finish off my necklace.

Storyteller: He ran after the Buddha. However, he couldn't catch him.

Angulimala: How is he moving so fast, stop, stop at once. I order you to stop and stand still.

(The Buddha turns around and looks at him in the eyes.)

Buddha: I am stopped. I am still. It is you that needs to stop and be still.

Angulimala: You can't fool me. I can see you moving.

Buddha: You don't understand, my friend. I am stopped, I am still because I don't harm people. I am kind and compassionate. You will never stop and you will never be still as long as you keep harming and killing people.

Angulimala: How dare you speak to me like that? Why are you not frightened of me? Don't you know who I am? I am Angulimala the great killer of men.

Buddha: My dear friend, the only thing that you need to kill is your hate.

Angulimala: Did you just call me a friend. No one has ever called me a friend before. What have I being doing?

Buddha: Come and be my friend. Come live with me and my friends. You will like it.

Angulimala: Are you sure?

Buddha: Yes I am sure. Follow me. It will be an adventure.

Angulimala: I love adventures. I will come with you and your friends.

(*Angulimala throws away his finger necklace and follows the Buddha.*)

Storyteller: That is how Angulimala, the terrible killer of men became a follower of the Buddha.

The moral is everyone can change their lives for the better.

A Cup of Tea

Characters: Storyteller, Buddha, a disciple, a cow and a man.

Storyteller: One day the Buddha and one of his discipleswere walking from town to town. They came across a lake.

Buddha: I'm very thirsty. Can you fetch me some water from that lake?

Disciple: Of course, Buddha.

(Buddha sat under a tree to mediate.)

Discple: I will fetch the water for us to drink as we have been walking all day and we are thirsrty.

(He gets a container and goes to the lake.)

Storyteller: Just as he was about to take some water a cow and cart splashes throught the lake.

Man: I'm sorry, cart has made the lake dirty. Please forgive me.

Disciple: The water is very dirty. We can't drink it. The Buddha will be disappointed.

(The disciple returns to the Buddha with an empty container.)

Disciple: I'm sorry but the water in the lake is very muddy. We can't drink or we will get sick.

Buddha: Don't worry. We can take a little rest and you can go back for the water later.

Storyteller: After an hour of rest the Buddha said...

Buddha: Go back and get some water for us to drink.

(The disciple went back to the lake.)

Disciple: The lake has got clear water. The Buddha was right, the mud has settled down and the water above it is clear. It looks good to drink.

(He quickly fills his container with water and returns to the Buddha.)

Buddha: You see if you let the water be, and the must settles down on its own and you got clear water that doesn't require any effort. It is the same thing with the mind too. When it is disturbed let it be. Just give it a little time. It will settle down on its own you don't need any effort to calm it down. We can judge and take the best decisions of our life when we stay calm.

Storyteller: Always stay calm and never make hasty decisions.

Other Books by the Author:

Drama Start Series:

Drama Start: Drama Activities, Plays and Monologues for Children (Ages 3-8).

Drama Start Two: Drama Activities for Children (Ages 9-12).

Stage Start: 20 Plays for Children (Ages 3-12).

Movement Start: Over 100 Movement Activities and Stories for Children.

ESL Drama Start: Drama Activities and Plays for ESL Learners.

On Stage Series:

Aesop's Fables on Stage: A Collection of Plays Based on Aesop's Fables.

Fairy Tales on Stage: A Collection of Plays for Children.

Classics on Stage: A Collection of Plays Based on Classic Children's Stories.

Christmas Stories on Stage: A Collection of Plays for Children.

Panchatantra on Stage: A Collection of Plays for Children.

Hans Christian Andersen's Stories on Stage: A Collection of Plays for Children.

Oscar Wilde's Stories on Stage: A Collection of Plays based on Oscar Wilde's Short Stories.

Just So Stories on Stage: A Collection of Plays based on Rudyard Kipling's Just So Stories.

Animal Stories on Stage: A Collection of Plays based on Animal Stories.

More Fairy Tales on Stage: A Collection of Plays based on Fairy Tales.

Irish Legends on Stage: A Collection of Plays based on Irish Legends.

Bible Stories on Stage: A Collection of Plays based on Bible Stories.

www.ingramcontent.com/pod-product-compliance
Lightning Source LLC
Chambersburg PA
CBHW020431010526
44118CB00010B/534